Decorate With Burlap

Whether your home is cottage chic or traditional, the natural look of modern and relaxed. Burlap's breezy charm and warm texture fit righ

Burlap is so easy and versatile you can sew it into curtains or cut it int appliqués for a garden wedding or shape it into roses for a rustic wrea ... even personalize it with stamps and stencils for sophisticated accents that are one-of-a-kind. Paired with basics like duck canvas and ticking, burlap has a timeless beauty that makes it a decorating classic.

Contents

LEISURE ARTS, INC.
Little Rock, Arkansas

Burlap

Burlap is a fabric made from a natural, bio-degradable fiber called Jute. It's rough fibrous texture and un-even weave make this a popular and unique fabric for all types of end uses.

Burlap is a crafter's dream. The threads remove easily to make a straight line for cutting or to create a channel for weaving a ribbon through. And with a zigzag stitch, it's a cinch to sew. This coarse fabric can be scrunched, ruffled, and frayed. It has tons of body and holds its shape. Woven with its own organic flaws, it is genuinely forgiving and fundamentally crafty. It comes in an array of colors and somehow goes with everything. Today's burlap is a home décor essential!

Tips & Tricks For Crafting With Burlap:

• To cut burlap in a straight line, mark the cut line with chalk and pull a thread out of the weave using a seam ripper.
• To keep edges from fraying, secure with liquid seam sealant.
• To intentionally fray an edge, remove two threads from the weave then secure with liquid seam sealant.
• To iron, use the cotton/wool setting and don't be afraid to use steam.
• To maintain burlap projects, spot clean only.

Duck Canvas & Ticking

Burlap's body and texture make it a natural for home decorating. And its down-to-earth nature is a perfect match for casually elegant duck canvas and ticking.

Duck Cloth is tough, and this durable 100% Cotton 9.3 oz./square yard fabric is really versatile. Duck Cloth's tight plain weave gives this fabric a lot of strength. This fabric is also called Canvas.

Ticking is a 100% Cotton twill weave, 6 oz./square yard. It is yarn-dyed, which makes the stripes "pop." It is very durable.

Tips & Tricks For Duck Canvas & Ticking:

- To prevent frayed edges, cut with pinking shears.
- To iron, use the cotton/wool setting and use steam if needed.
- To protect duck and ticking projects, spray them with a fabric protector like Scotchgard™.
- When sewing two pieces of ticking together, remember to line up the stripes.

Ruffled Rose Wreath

Rustic burlap gets the ruffle treatment on this welcoming rose wreath.

Supplies:
18" grapevine wreath
1/4 yard natural burlap
1/4 yard royal blue burlap
1/4 yard hunter green burlap
1/4 yard sage burlap
6 rhinestone & brass flower
 shank buttons, 1"
natural embroidery floss
royal blue embroidery floss
hunter green embroidery floss
sage embroidery floss
liquid seam sealant
 (like Dritz® Fray Check™)

Tools:
iron
hot glue & glue gun
scissors
seam ripper
embroidery needle
tape measure

1. To make a large rose, cut a 3" by 36" strip of natural burlap. To get a straight line, mark where you want to cut and pull a thread out of the burlap weave using a seam ripper. Fold the strip of burlap in half lengthwise and press with an iron. Run a bead of liquid seam sealant along the cut edges and let dry.

2. Fold one corner over and sew along the cut edges using a 46" piece of embroidery floss and a 1" running stitch. Keep the needle and floss attached. Pull the floss to ruffle the burlap, then roll the burlap around itself to make a rose. Sew back and forth at the base of the rose. Repeat to make five more large roses: two royal blue, two hunter green, and one sage.

3. To make the small roses, use the same technique with 2" by 24" strips of burlap. Make three natural, two royal blue, and two sage.

4. Hot glue four large roses along the lower right of the wreath and two large roses on the upper left. Flank these with small roses, then tuck the rest of the roses in the gaps between, securing with hot glue. Hot glue a shank button in the center of each large rose.

TIP
Burlap tends to unravel, so don't cut until you're ready to craft. Frayed edges may be part of its charm, but liquid seam sealant will keep rough edges from fraying too much.

Burlap-Banded Pillow

Earthy burlap gets chic with an ornate stamp and woven satin trim.

Supplies:

14" x 28" pillow form
1/2 yard navy duck canvas
1/2 yard navy ticking
1/3 yard natural burlap
1/3 yard osnaburg
1 3/4 yard navy satin ribbon, 3/8" wide
5" fleur-de-lis foam stamp
navy acrylic paint
liquid seam sealant
 (like Dritz® Fray Check™)
navy thread
natural thread

Tools:

sewing machine
iron
scissors
pinking shears
seam ripper
sewing needle
straight pins
safety pin
foam paintbrush
tape measure

1. Cut two pieces of navy duck 15" by 15". Cut two pieces of navy ticking 15" by 15". To make the front, sew one ticking square and one duck square together using a 1/2" seam allowance, stitching parallel to the stripe. Repeat with the remaining squares to make the back. Press seam allowances open.

2. Lay the two pieces face to face with the fabrics matching each other. Pin all the way around the edge and sew together with a 1/2" seam, leaving a 10" opening along one edge for inserting the pillow form. Sew a few stitches in reverse at the beginning and end of the seams to lock them in place. Turn the pillow right side out and insert the pillow form. Hand sew the opening closed using a ladder stitch. (See diagram on page 31.)

3. Cut a 9" by 31" piece of burlap. Remove two threads from the long edges to fray them. Secure with liquid seam sealant.

4. Lay the burlap on a piece of scrap paper. Paint the surface of the foam stamp with navy paint and stamp onto the center of the burlap band. Let dry.

5. Measure 1/2" in from the long frayed edge of the burlap band and use the seam ripper to remove enough burlap threads to weave the ribbon through. Attach a safety pin to the end of a 31" piece of ribbon and use it to weave the ribbon in and out of the open weave. (See Photo 1.)
Repeat for the other side of the burlap band.

6. Back the burlap band with an 8" by 31" piece of osnaburg cut with pinking shears. Wrap the lined burlap band around the pillow inside out and pin the ends together through all the layers. Slide off the pillow. Sew together with a zigzag stitch. Turn the band right side out and slide back onto the pillow.

Photo 1

Monogrammed Table Runner

Set the table for elegance with a personalized runner featuring a Deco monogram.

Supplies:

2¹/₄ yards white burlap
5¹/₄ yards black twill tape, 1" wide
3¹/₂" upper case alphabet stencil set
  (like FolkArt® Stencil Décor® Victorian Alphabet)
3" ornate corner stencil
  (like Americana® Classic™ Stencils)
³/₄" Spouncer™ or stenciling sponge
black acrylic paint
fabric glue
  (like Beacon Adhesives™ Fabri-Tac™)

Tools:

iron
scissors
seam ripper
masking tape
tape measure
chalk

1. Measure the length of your table and add 9" to each end for the drops. The runner for our 60" table will be 78" long. The width will be 13", which is standard.

2. Straight lines are important for this runner, so before cutting the burlap, mark your dimensions with chalk and pull a thread out of the weave using a seam ripper. Use this as a cutting guide for each side of the runner.

3. To monogram the runner, center a letter stencil on the 9" drop and secure with masking tape. Slide a scrap piece of paper beneath the burlap. Dab small amounts of paint into the openings of the stencil using the Spouncer™, being careful not to get paint underneath the edges. (A straight up and down motion works best.) Let dry. Use the same technique for the two corner stencils and let dry. Repeat to monogram the drop on the other end of the runner.

4. To edge the runner, fold the twill tape in half lengthwise and iron. Slide the folded twill tape onto the edge of the runner and glue into place. When you get to a corner, trim the twill tape flush with the runner and start again in the new direction, gluing as you go.

TIP

We used one long piece of burlap, which leaves a lot fabric left over. To save on yardage, buy one yard, cut it into three 13" long pieces, and glue them together, covering the seams with ribbon or trim.

Cheers Wine Bag

A handmade bag makes a gift of wine even more special. Cheers to that!

Supplies:
$1/2$ yard gold burlap
$3/4$ yard burgundy satin ribbon, $5/8$" wide
1" black iron-on letters set
 (like Dritz® Iron-on Letters™ Monogram)
gold thread

Tools:
iron
scissors
seam ripper
sewing needle
straight pins
safety pin
ruler

1. Cut a 12" by 18" piece of burlap. Cut the letters to spell C H E E R S out of the iron-on letter sheets. Lay the burlap down so the short side is nearest to you. Arrange the letters face down on the burlap vertically with the C 8" from the top, the S 3" from the bottom, and all the letters centered 6" from each side. Iron each letter into place following the directions on the package. (See diagram on page 29.)

2. Turn the burlap face down. Fold the top edge over 1" and iron a crease. Fold the edge over again 3" and iron. Pin the hem in place, then hand sew with a backstitch. (See diagram on page 31.)

3. Wrap the burlap inside out around a wine bottle and pin the long sides together in a straight line at the widest part of the bottle. Slide the wine bottle out and sew the seam together with a backstitch. Sew the bottom edges together with a $1/2$" seam. Turn the wine bag right side out.

4. Measure $2^3/4$" from the top hemmed edge and remove a thread from the burlap using the seam ripper. Remove four or five more threads and weave the ribbon through. (See page 6.) Attach a safety pin to the end of the ribbon and use it to weave the ribbon in and out of the open weave, starting directly above the word CHEERS. As you weave, go under three strands of burlap about every $1^1/2$".

5. Slide the wine bottle into the bag. Tuck the bottom corners under the wine bottle and stitch together. Cinch the bag closed with the ribbon and tie in a bow.

TIP
Make this wine bag with a message like "JOY" to dress up a wine bottle as a holiday gift!

Pocketed Message Board

Give a utilitarian corkboard a Paris flea market makeover with grain-sack stencils and a yardstick frame.

Supplies:
23" x 35" wood-framed corkboard
1 yard natural burlap
²/₃ yard red burlap
¹/₃ yard brown burlap
3¹/₃ yards red grosgrain ribbon, ⁵/₈" wide
4 wooden yardsticks
1¹/₂" alphabet stencil set
3" rooster stencil
1" flourish stencil
³/₄" Spouncer™ or stenciling sponge
black acrylic paint
water-based wood stain
 (like Oak FolkArt® Stain)
clear acrylic sealer
fusible bonding tape, ⁵/₈"
 (like Dritz® Stitch Witchery™)
fabric glue (like Beacon Adhesives™
 Fabri-Tac™)

Tools:
iron & pressing cloth
handsaw
staple gun & staples
scissors
masking tape
foam paintbrush
tape measure
sponge
chalk

1. Remove the frame from the corkboard. Cut a piece of natural burlap 28" by 40". Cover the corkboard with the burlap and staple on the back. To wrap the corners, fold the burlap like you are wrapping a present and staple on the back.

2. Arrange the stencils on the top half of the message board and mark their placement with chalk. As you go, tape each stencil in place and dab small amounts of black paint into the openings using the Spouncer™. Be careful not to get paint underneath the edges. Let dry. Repeat until your design is complete. Remove the chalk with a damp sponge.

3. To make a pocket, cut a piece of red burlap 26" by 9". Follow manufacturer's instructions to iron a 1" double-hemmed cuff in the long side using fusible bonding tape and a pressing cloth. Flip the burlap over and iron a 1" fold along the other long side. Cut and cuff three pockets, two red and one brown.

4. Attach the top pocket halfway down the message board. To do this, lay the red pocket on the board and hold the bottom 1" fold in place. Flip the pocket down out of the way and staple the 1" fold to the message board. Flip the pocket back up, wrap it around the sides, and staple in back. Overlap the bottom of the pocket with the brown pocket by 2" and attach in the same way. Repeat to attach the other red pocket.

5. Cut the yardsticks to fit around the message board using a handsaw. (Or have them cut at the hardware store.) Paint the yardsticks with a mixture of half oak stain and half clear sealant. Let dry.
Glue the yardsticks around the message board.
Glue red ribbon around the outside edge of the message board.

LES POULETS

de
PROVENCE

Grommeted Café Curtains

Curtains may seem like a big project, but burlap makes it easy. And once you iron the header, the grommets literally go on in a snap!

Supplies for two 29" x 22" curtain panels:
2 yards natural burlap
$1/2$ yard oyster burlap, 46" wide
2 yards red grosgrain ribbon, $1^1/2$" wide
12 snap-together curtain grommets with
  template, 1" (like Dritz® Home Grommets)
$1/3$ yard fusible web, 17" wide
  (like Steam-A-Seam®)
liquid seam sealant
  (like Dritz® Fray Check™)
off-white embroidery floss
red thread
natural thread

Tools:
sewing machine
iron & pressing cloth
scissors
pinking shears
sewing needle
embroidery needle
straight pins
tape measure
chalk

To Make Each Panel
1. Measure your window for café curtains following the directions on page 28. Cut a piece of natural burlap to your cut fabric size. Iron a double $1/2$" hem along the side of the panel. Machine sew with a zigzag stitch. At the beginning and end of each hem, sew a few stitches in reverse to lock them in place. Repeat to double-hem the other side.

2. Iron a $1/2$" hem in the bottom of the panel, then fold the hem over 4" and iron flat. Sew with a zigzag stitch.

3. To create a header sturdy enough for grommets, iron a $1/2$" hem in the top of the panel, then fold the hem over 3" and iron flat. Line the hem with fusible web and iron with a damp pressing cloth. Sew with a zigzag stitch.

4. Cut a 7" strip of oyster burlap twice the width of your panel. Seal the edges with liquid seam sealant. Hand sew a 1" running stitch down the center using a 40" piece of embroidery floss. Pull the floss to create a ruffle in the burlap until the piece shortens to the width of your panel.

5. Cut a piece of ribbon the length of the ruffle with pinking shears and dab the ends with liquid seam sealant. Pin the ribbon to the center of the ruffle, then sew with red thread and a zigzag stitch. Hand sew the center line of the ruffle to the curtain with natural thread, hiding the stitches in the burlap behind the ribbon.

6. Evenly space the grommets across the top of the panel with the first and last grommets $1^1/2$" from the sides. Mark the grommet holes with chalk using the template that comes with the grommets. Cut a hole for each grommet and snap the grommets in place following the directions on the package.

TIP
Grommets come in all kinds of colors and finishes. Select a set that closely matches the curtain rod and hardware where you want to hang your curtains.

Toile Bolster

This dramatic bolster is actually a no-sew project. Who knew?!

Supplies:
9" x 20" bolster pillow form
1 yard black duck canvas
1 yard black and ivory toile
2 yards jute rope
fusible bonding tape, $^5/_8$"
 (like Dritz® Stitch Witchery™)

Tools:
iron & pressing cloth
scissors
straight pins
2 rubber bands
clear tape
tacky glue
tape measure

1. Cut a 30" by 40" piece of black duck. Follow manufacturers instructions to iron a 1" hem in the short ends of the duck using fusible bonding tape and a damp pressing cloth.

2. Wrap the duck around the pillow form inside out and pin the unfinished edges together. Remove the pillow form and fuse that seam together using fusible bonding tape, following manufacturers instructions. Remove the pins. Turn the duck right side out.

3. Slide the pillow form into the duck. Gather each end and secure with a rubber band, then wrap with 1 yard of jute rope three times and tie in a knot. Snip off the rubber bands. Wrap clear tape around the ends of the rope where you want to trim, cut through the tape and rope, then dab tacky glue on each end to prevent fraying. Let dry, then remove the tape.

4. Lay out the toile and select the area you want to show on the band. Centering the area you want to show, cut a band 18" wide x 30" long. Iron a 1" hem in the long sides of the toile using fusible bonding tape and a damp pressing cloth.

5. Wrap the band around the pillow inside out and pin the unfinished edges together, then slide the band off. Lay fusible bonding tape along the seam and iron with a pressing cloth. Turn the band right side out and slide it onto the pillow.

Stenciled Vanity Stool

Turn plain canvas into a designer textile for a stylish vanity stool that's one-of-a-kind.

Supplies:
vanity stool with removable seat
$^2/_3$ yard natural duck canvas
6" clock face stencil*
6" numbers stencil*
6" key & script stencil*
$^3/_4$" Spouncer™ or stenciling sponge
black acrylic paint
 *we used 6x6 Template Minis from
 The Crafter's Workshop

Tools:
staple gun & staples
screwdriver
scissors
masking tape
tape measure
chalk

1. Remove the seat from the stool with a screwdriver and set the screws aside. Lightly trace the seat onto the duck with chalk. Cut a circle out of the duck 3" bigger than the chalk outline.

2. Protect your work surface. Lay the stencils out on the duck using masking tape to hold them in place. Dab small amounts of paint into the openings of each stencil using the Spouncer™. Be careful not to get paint beneath the edges. Let dry.

3. Wash and dry the stencils, reposition them on the duck, and spounce through them again. Vary the direction of the stencils each time, and don't be afraid to use different sections of the stencils. Let dry.

4. Cover the seat with the stenciled duck. To staple on the back, start with four staples opposite each other. Pull the duck taut and continue stapling all the way around the seat. Place the seat back on the stool and secure with screws.

TIP
Look for a vintage vanity stool at garage sales or thrift stores and give it a facelift with a fresh coat of spray paint before covering the seat.

Felt-Appliquéd Pillow

Make a keepsake pillow with a charming bunny appliqué complete with a button-eye and a pom-pom tail!

Supplies:
12" x 12" pillow form
$^1/_2$ yard green duck canvas
$^1/_4$ yard white felt
1 sheet of fusible web, 9" x 12"
 (like Steam-A-Seam2®)
$^1/_2$ yard blue & white
polka dot ribbon, $^3/_8$" wide
2" white pompom
$^3/_8$" light blue button
navy embroidery floss
khaki thread
white thread
blue thread

Tools:
sewing machine
iron & pressing cloth
scissors
sewing needle
embroidery needle
straight pins
tape measure

1. Cut two pieces of duck 13" by 13". Stack the pieces together and pin all the way around the edge. Sew together with a $^1/_2$" seam, leaving a 10" opening along one edge for inserting the pillow form. Sew a few stitches in reverse at the beginning and end of the seams to lock them in place. Turn the cover right side out.

2. Using the template on page 29, cut the bunny shape out of the white felt. Starting at the bunny's tail, blanket-stitch the entire edge of the felt bunny with navy embroidery floss. (See blanket-stitch diagram on page 31.)

3. Use the same template to cut the bunny shape out of the fusible web. Layer the felt bunny over the fusible-web bunny and iron onto the center of the pillow cover with a damp pressing cloth. Make sure the opening of the cover is at the bottom.

4. Sew the pompom onto the bunny appliqué. Tie the blue and white polka dot ribbon into a bow. Sew it to the bunny's neck. Use navy embroidery floss to sew on the button eye.

5. Slide the pillow form into the cover. Sew the opening closed using a ladder stitch. (See diagram on page 31.)

TIP
Make a whole set of forest-friend pillows with squirrel, deer, and raccoon appliqués cut from different colors of felt!

Ticking & Canvas Tote

Red canvas and ticking are a perfect match in this rope-handled tote.

Supplies:
$^1/_2$ yard red duck canvas
$^1/_2$ yard red ticking
2 yards white soft cotton rope
4 silver grommets & setter, $^7/_{16}$" diameter
red thread

Tools:
sewing machine
hammer
scissors
sewing needle
straight pins
tape measure
chalk

1. Cut two pieces of duck 16" by 16". Cut two pieces of ticking 16" by 16". Sew one ticking square and one duck square together using a $^1/_2$" seam allowance, stitching perpendicular to the stripe. Repeat with remaining squares. Press seam allowances open.

2. Lay the two pieces face to face with the fabrics matching each other. Pin all the way around the edge and sew together with a $^1/_2$" seam, leaving a 3" opening in the ticking side for turning the fabric right side out.

3. To give the bottom of the tote a boxed shape, match side and bottom seams. Draw a chalk line perpendicular to the seams 3" from the corner, then machine sew. Cut off the excess fabric. Repeat for all four corners.

4. Turn the piece right side out, then sew the 3" gap closed using a ladder stitch. Tuck the ticking into the duck as a liner. Fold the top edge of the ticking over to create a $1^1/_2$" wide lip. (See diagram on page 31.)

5. Use chalk to mark the grommet holes, centering them on the lip $4^1/_2$" from the side seams. Cut and set the grommets using the grommet setter and a hammer, following the directions on the package.

6. Cut the rope in half. Feed the ends through the grommets, securing each end with a knot.

TIP
To keep your tote looking brand new for years to come, spray it with a fabric protector like Scotchguard™!

Sweetheart Pennant Banner

Create a sweet and simple pennant banner to spread the love of burlap!

Supplies:
1/2 yard natural burlap
1/4 yard denim
1/4 yard navy ticking
1/4 yard red ticking
1/4 yard red & white calico
1/4 yard red & white plaid calico
1 2/3 yards natural braided jute rope
5 shell buttons, 5/8"
liquid seam sealant
 (like Dritz® Fray Check™)
fabric glue
 (like Beacon Adhesives™ Fabri-Tac™)

Tools:
scissors
pinking shears

1. Using the pattern on page 30, cut five burlap triangles with regular scissors. Seal the edges with liquid seam sealant. Let dry.

2. Using the large heart pattern on page 30, cut five hearts out of denim with regular scissors. Use the small heart template and pinking shears to cut two hearts out of the plaid calico, one out of each ticking, and one out of the print calico.

3. Fold the top 1" of a triangle pennant over the rope at the center. Glue in place, then trim any burlap that peeks out from the back. Glue two pennants on each side of the center one. Let dry.

4. Center and glue a denim heart topped with patterned heart and a button on each pennant.

5. Cut six 5" long strips out of the leftover denim and calico, then tie onto the rope in simple knots between each pennant.

NOTE:
The supplies listed are for a banner approximately 40" in length from the left end of the rope to the right end of the rope.

TIP

Make this darling banner with pastel colors to shower a baby with love.
You can make this banner as long as you'd like! Just add more pennants on each side.

Appliquéd Candleholder

Dress up an ordinary candleholder with natural burlap embellished with lace and pearls.

Supplies:
glass candleholder, 7$\frac{1}{4}$" tall, 3$\frac{1}{2}$" diameter
white pillar candle, 5$\frac{1}{2}$" tall, 2$\frac{3}{4}$" diameter
white lace rose appliqué, 5" x 3"
$\frac{1}{4}$ yard natural burlap
$\frac{2}{3}$ yard white lace beaded trim
21 self-adhesive half-pearls, $\frac{1}{8}$"
fabric glue
 (like Beacon Adhesives™ Fabri-Tac™)

Tools:
scissors
ruler

1. Cut an 11$\frac{1}{2}$" by 4" piece of burlap.

2. Apply fabric glue to the back of the appliqué and press into the center of the burlap. Be sure to protect your work surface as the glue may seep through the open weave of the burlap.

3. Cut the lace trim into two 11$\frac{1}{2}$" strips. Glue the strips to the top and bottom edges of the burlap.

4. Embellish the area around the appliqué with trios of half-pearls.

5. Wrap the embellished burlap around the candleholder so it overlaps in the back. Secure with fabric glue. Place the pillar candle inside.

TIP
These elegant candleholders are ideal for a wedding
The materials are inexpensive, and you can make dozens of them in a flash!

Measuring For Café Curtains

Measuring for Café Curtains

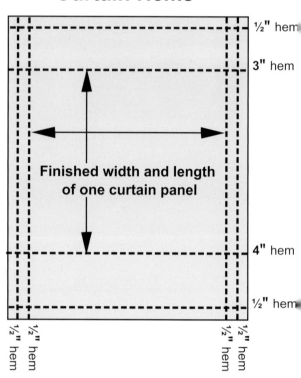

window

↕ +1½"

window width

+3"   +3"

desired drop

Multiply width by 2 to account for fullness
Divide that measurement by 2 to make two curtain panels

Curtain Hems

½" hem

3" hem

**Finished width and length
of one curtain panel**

4" hem

½" hem

½" hem   ½" hem   ½" hem   ½" hem

Measuring For Café Curtains

1. For the finished width of your curtains, measure the width of your window and add 3" to each side. Double this width to create fullness. If two curtain panels are desired, divide by 2.

2. To get the finished length of your curtains, measure from $1^1/_2$" above the rod down to your desired length.

3. Add the following hem allowances to your finished measurements to get the cut fabric size. To the width, add 2" for each panel. To the length, add 8" for the top and bottom hems.

Diagrams and Patterns

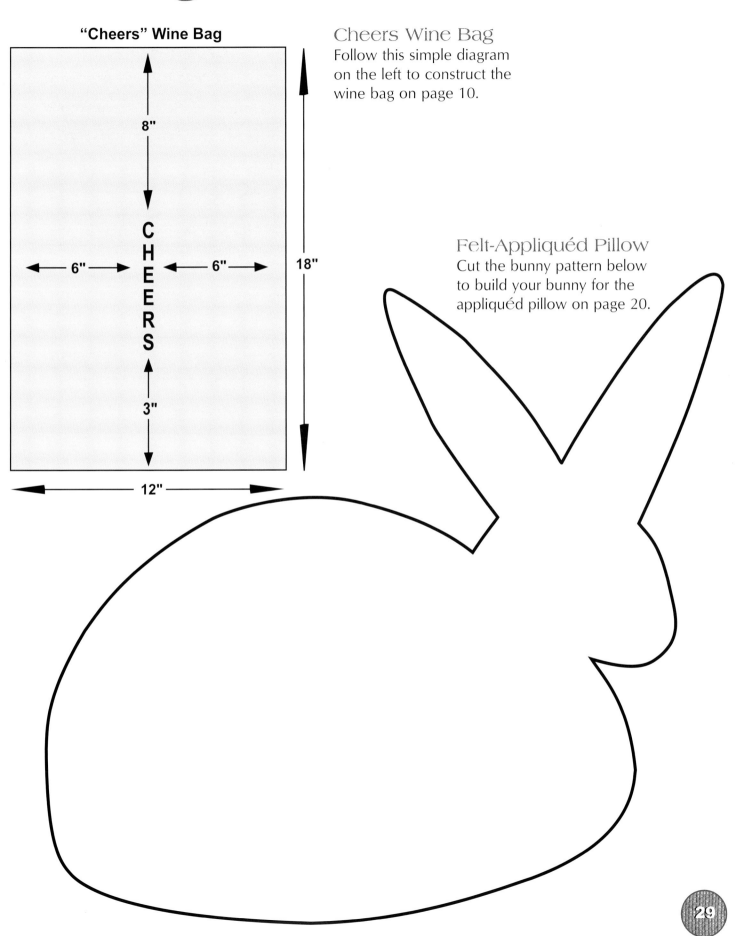

"Cheers" Wine Bag

8"

C
H
E
E
R
S

6"   6"

18"

3"

12"

Cheers Wine Bag
Follow this simple diagram
on the left to construct the
wine bag on page 10.

Felt-Appliquéd Pillow
Cut the bunny pattern below
to build your bunny for the
appliquéd pillow on page 20.

Sweetheart Pennant Banner Patterns

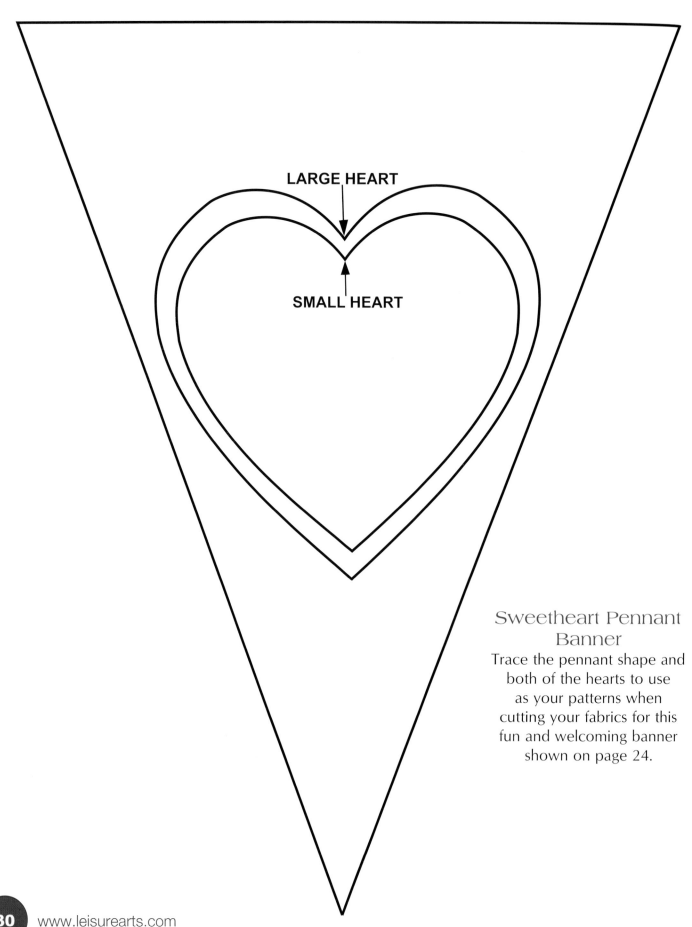

LARGE HEART

SMALL HEART

Sweetheart Pennant Banner

Trace the pennant shape and both of the hearts to use as your patterns when cutting your fabrics for this fun and welcoming banner shown on page 24.

Hand Sewing & Embroidery Stitches

When using the Ladder Stitch:

Bring the needle up at 1 and go down at 2 into the fold. Pulling the folds together as you work, come up at 3 and all odd numbers, and go down at 4 and all even numbers.

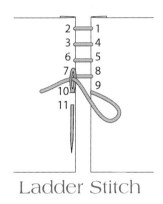

Ladder Stitch

When using the Backstitch:

Come up at 1, go down at 2, and come up at 3. Continuing in the same manner and forming a continuous line, go down at 4, come up at 5, and go down at 6.

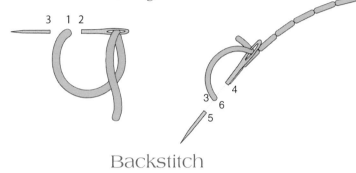

Backstitch

When using the Blanket Stitch:

Bring the needle up at 1. Keeping the thread below the point of the needle, go down at 2 and come up at 3. Continue working in the same manner, going down at even numbers and coming up at odd numbers.

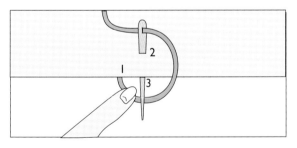

Blanket Stitch–View 1

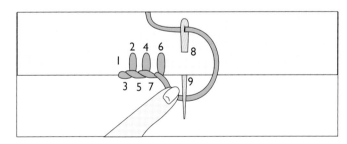

Blanket Stitch–View 2

CREDITS

CRAFT PROJECTS & PHOTOGRAPHY BY

Jennifer & Kitty O'Neil
www.ONeilSisters.com

GRAPHIC DESIGNER

Kathleen Young

We have made every effort to ensure that these instructions are accurate and complete. We cannot, however, be responsible for human error, typographical mistakes, or variations in individual work.

LEISURE ARTS
the art of everyday living
www.leisurearts.com

All Burlap, Duck, and Ticking fabrics shown in projects in this book are from James Thompson & Co., Inc. and are available at fabric and craft retailers everywhere!

JAMES THOMPSON
Est. 1860
& CO. INC.

PRODUCTION MANAGER

Bob Humphrey